The Rebellion:—Its Origin and Main-Spring.

AN ORATION

DELIVERED BY

HON. CHARLES SUMNER

UNDER THE AUSPICES OF THE

YOUNG MEN'S REPUBLICAN UNION OF NEW YORK,

NOVEMBER 27, 1861.

NEW YORK:
PRINTED FOR THE YOUNG MEN'S REPUBLICAN UNION,

1861.

YOUNG MEN'S REPUBLICAN UNION,

Organized June, 1856, as the "FREMONT & DAYTON CENTRAL UNION."

HEAD-QUARTERS, STUYVESANT INSTITUTE, 659 Broadway, New York.

This organization was the first in the country to inscribe the name of LINCOLN on its banner, and the first to ratify the Chicago nominations in New York. It organized the first company of Wide-Awakes in the Empire State, and published and circulated 3,961,000 pages of Campaign documents, among which were the Illustrated Life of Lincoln, in German, and Mr. Lincoln's Cooper Institute Speech, with notes.

Officers of the Union.

CHARLES T. RODGERS, *President*,
DEXTER A. HAWKINS, *Vice-President*,
ERASMUS STERLING, *Secretary*,
WILLIAM M. FRANKLIN, *Treasurer*.

Executive Committee.

CEPHAS BRAINERD, *Chairman*,
BENJAMIN F. MANIERRE,
CHARLES C. NOTT,
FRANK W. BALLARD,
THOMAS L. THORNELL,
JAMES H. WELSH,
E. C. JOHNSON,
CHARLES H. COOPER,
P. G. DEGRAW,
LEWIS M. PECK.

Advisory Board.

WM. CULLEN BRYANT,
HON. HORACE GREELEY,
HON. HAMILTON FISH,
HON. HIRAM BARNEY,
HON. WILLIAM V. BRADY,
DANIEL DREW,
HON. BENJAMIN F. MANIERRE,
FRANCIS HALL,
HON. CHARLES A. PEABODY,
RICHARD C. McCORMICK,
WILLIAM CURTIS NOYES,
HON. GEORGE FOLSOM,
JAMES KELLY,
EDGAR KETCHUM,
GEORGE W. BLUNT,
HON. ABIJAH MANN, JR.
HENRY A. HURLBUT.

The Rebellion:—Its Origin and Main-Spring.

AN ORATION

Delivered before the Citizens of New York,

UNDER THE AUSPICES OF

The New York Young Men's Republican Union,

AT COOPER INSTITUTE,

ON WEDNESDAY EVENING, NOV. 27, 1861,

BY HON. CHARLES SUMNER,

UNITED STATES' SENATOR FROM MASSACHUSETTS.

THE assemblage before which this oration was delivered was remarkable in numbers and in character. Long before the hour named for the meeting, the immense hall was crowded, and notwithstanding that the evening was stormy, the proportion of ladies present was larger than ever before seen in New York on such an occasion.

Upon the platform were seated many distinguished Americans, among whom may be named Hon. William Pennington, Ex-Governor of New Jersey, and Ex-Speaker of the House of Representatives; Hon. Schuyler Colfax, of Indiana; Hon. Lot C. Morrill, of Vermont; Charles King, LL.D., President of Columbia College; Professor Francis Lieber; David Dudley Field, Esq., William M. Evarts, Esq., John Jay, Esq., Rev. Stephen H. Tyng, D.D., Rev. William Hague, D.D., Rev. George B. Cheever, D.D., Rev. Theodore L. Cuyler, Rev. Alfred Cookman, John H. Griscom, M.D., Hon. John W. Edmonds, Gen. Prosper M. Wetmore, Lewis Tappan, Rev. William Goodell, Hon. Charles A. Peabody, Rev. Roswell D. Hitchcock, D.D., Rev. Henry M. Field, Hon. Thomas B. Stillman, Hon. Benjamin F. Manierre, R. M. Blatchford, Esq., William Pitt Palmer, Esq., D. A. Harsha, Esq., George P. Putnam, Esq., Elliott C. Cowdin, Esq., Hon. William B. Taylor, Postmaster of New York, Hon. Rufus F. Andrews, Surveyor of the Port, Hon. H. B. Stanton, Deputy Collector, Hon. Joseph Hoxie, Major A. A. Selover, U. S. Army, Oliver Johnson, Esq.

Charles T. Rodgers, Esq., President of the "Union," introduced William Curtis Noyes, Esq., as the presiding officer of the meeting, and a list of Vice-Presidents and Secretaries was unanimously adopted.

Mr. NOYES, upon taking the chair, delivered the following address:—

LADIES AND GENTLEMEN:—Thanking you, as I do, gratefully for the kindness which has called me to preside over this meeting, let me remind you that within the modest chapel which impresses with devotional emotions every visitor to Mount Auburn—that most beautiful of American cemeteries—stands a marble statue of one of the patriot leaders of the American Revolution. Its simple dignity arrests attention and commands admiration and respect. Stern resolve and unflinching courage are depicted in lineament and attitude. We see him voluntarily renouncing a high professional office under the crown to take his place in the forum as a private citizen, to oppose, without reward, the odious violations of the liberties of the people by means of writs of assistance. His exordium startles the prejudiced judges:—

> Let the consequences be what they will, I am determined to proceed. The only principles of public conduct that are worthy of a gentleman or a man, are to sacrifice estate, ease, health, and applause, and even life, to the sacred calls of country. These principles, in private life, make the good citizen; in public life, the patriot and the hero.

Then, rising with the progress of his great theme, he continues:—

> Every man in a state of nature is an independent sovereign, subject to no law but the law written upon his heart and revealed to him by his Maker. His right to his life, his liberty, and his property, no created being can rightfully contest; these rights are inherent and inalienable.

We watch the effect of his indignant words—they convince and awe, and yet the royal tribunal dare not decide. It prevaricates and postpones, but the victory is won; the odious measure is abandoned for ever, and the orator's utterances have lighted up a flame which independence alone can ever quench.

We go with him from this first theatre of triumph through many long years of toil and anxiety, in shaping the measures which led to the great conflict with the mother country, to the General Court, guided by his skill and political sagacity; to the popular assembly alike aroused to turbulence and hushed to repose by his burning eloquence. We see him hurling defiance at the minions of power who, with secret malevolence, assailed his reputation. We witness their malignant hatred, and their deadly assault upon his person when alone and unarmed. We see him fall, covered with wounds, and carried bleeding to his home.

Thenceforward, to the actual opening of the Revolutionary drama, and during its progress, this act of regal barbarism obscured, but did not wholly extinguish, the light of the great intellect which it sought to destroy, but all that remained was a wreck, reminding only of the glories of the past. The crime against the person added to its atrocity a greater crime against the soul, dooming it to pursue its earthly career in sadness and gloom. Conscious of being only a monument of decay, well might the gradually expiring patriot wish that when God, in his righteous Providence, should call him from time into eternity, it might be by a flash of lightning. We may rejoice that his prayer was answered, and that—too noble to be permitted to die a common death—in a manner equally affecting and sublime, JAMES OTIS (applause) was removed to the mansions of eternal felicity.

It is the necessary result of barbarism, in all its phases, to furnish historic parallels by reproducing itself in viler forms. Not a century elapsed, and a similar atrocity is enacted in the Senate Chamber of the United States. The ruffians were actuated by as deadly a hate, their malice was as foul and murderous, their defiance of law was as manifest, their victim was also the friend and advocate of universal freedom, and as much distinguished and feared, and he also fell beneath the blows of assassins in heart and conduct.

But here the parallel ends. This outrage did not impair the intellect which it sought to destroy; that survived the trial—enlarged, strengthened, purified—to set forward in a new and more glorious career in the cause of freedom and humanity. Instead of the lightning's flash to remove it to heaven, a divine influence, equal in potency, has emanated thence, inspiring it with a larger love of freedom, more zeal in the cause of the oppressed, and a more earnest conviction that human slavery produces only evil, and that it should be forever eradicated. (Enthusiastic applause.)

Happy, then, for us, and for our country, has been the suffering of these martyrs in the cause of freedom. The name of James Otis has descended to posterity on the brightest pages of our history, associated with those of Hancock, and Adams, and Jay, and Jefferson, and Henry, and Rutledge, and there it will remain forever.

The name of that other martyr in the cause of truth and justice, will find equal distinction in future ages on the roll of philanthropists, with those of Howard, and Clarkson, and Wilberforce, and others of that glorious company, "of whom the world was not worthy."

But history has also its retributions. The infamous actors in these tragedies passed away under the scorn and contempt of mankind, their names only searched for and remembered among the persecutors and slayers of their race. They who countenanced and approved the last—by a fitting gradation—became the betrayers and assassins of their country, and two of these—the highest in station and basest in conduct—are now awaiting the punishment due to their crimes in a prison within the shadow of Bunker Hill Monument, (applause,) which indignantly frowns upon them from base to summit.

In the reality of the present, behold the promise of the future, when all traitors like them shall meet a similar doom. Still devoting himself to the cause of his country and to the freedom of the oppressed, the advocate and friend of all, of whatever rank or condition of color, the scholar, the philanthropist, the martyr, the statesman, has come again among us, and it is with equal pride and pleasure that I present to you the Hon. Charles Sumner, not of Massachusetts, but of the United States of America, one and indivisible.

Mr. Sumner then came forward, and was received by the vast audience with tumultuous applause, in which the ladies joined with every manifestation of delight. The cheers, and waving of hats, and handkerchiefs lasted several minutes.

At the conclusion of Mr. Sumner's oration, the following resolutions were offered and adopted by acclamation:

Resolved, That the doctrine enunciated by Major-General Fremont with respect to the emancipation of the slaves of rebels, and the more recent utterances of General Burnside, Senator Wilson, and the Hon. George Bancroft, in this city; and of Col. John Cochrane and the Hon. Simon Cameron at Washington, foreshadowing the eventual rooting out of slavery, as the cause of the rebellion, indicate alike a moral, political, and military necessity; and, in the judgment of this meeting, the public sentiment of the North is now fully in sympathy with any practicable scheme which may be presented for the extirpation of this national evil, and will accept such result as the only consistent issue of this contest between civilization and barbarism.

Resolved, That the thanks of this meeting be, and are hereby, tendered to the Hon. Charles Sumner, the distinguished orator of this evening, for his reassertion and eloquent enforcement of the political principle herein indorsed.

SPEECH OF HON. CHARLES SUMNER.

Mr. President:—It is my nature to be more touched by the kindness of friends than by the malignity of enemies; and I know something of both. You make me feel that I am among friends. It gives me much pleasure to be welcomed by the Republican Union, first, as you represent the young men who are the hope and strength of the country, and, secondly, as you constitute an association which has already rendered signal service in saving the country from the rule of the Slave Oligarchy. It was under your auspices, that our candidate for the Presidency, known and honored in Illinois, became equally known and honored in New York. Nor is it too much to say that the masterly speech which he made at your invitation in this very hall, was needed to complete those titles to regard which caused his nomination at Chicago, and his election by the people. It was he who did the work; but you supplied the opportunity.

Fellow-Citizens of New York:—

In the presence of such an audience, so genial and almost so festive in character—assembled for no purpose of party or even of politics, in the ordinary sense of that term—I incline naturally to some topic of literature, of history, of science, of art,—to something, at least, which makes for peace. But at this moment, when our whole continent is beginning to shake with the tread of mustering armies, the voice refuses any such theme. The ancient poet, longing to sing of Achilles and the house of Atreus, found that he could only sing of love,—and he snatched from his lyre its bloody string. Alas! for me the case is all changed. I can speak to you only of war; but do not forget that if I speak of war, it is because unhappily war has become to us the only way of peace.

The present is too apt to appear trivial and unimportant, while the past and the future are grand. Rarely do men know the full significance of the period in which they live, and we are all inclined to sigh for something better in the way of opportunity—such as was given to the hero of the past, or such as our imagination allots to the better hero of the future. But there is no occasion for such repining now. There is nothing in the past, and it is difficult to imagine any thing in the future, more inspiring than our present. Even with the curtain yet slightly lifted, it is easy to see that events are now gathering, which, in their development, must constitute the third great epoch in the history of this Western Hemisphere;—the first being its discovery by Christopher Columbus, and the second being the American Revolution. And now it remains to be seen that this epoch of ours may not surpass in grandeur either of its two predecessors, so that the fame of the Discoverer and the fame of the Liberator—of Columbus and of Washington—may be eclipsed by the mild effulgence beaming from an act of god-like justice, which, within its immediate influence, will create a new heaven and a new earth, while in other lands its life-giving example will be felt so long as men struggle for rights denied, so long as any human being wears a chain.

War is always an epoch. Unhappily, history counts by wars. Of these, some have been wars of ideas—like that between the Catholics and Huguenots in France; between the Catholics and Protestants in Germany; between the arbitrary crown of Charles I. and the Puritanism of Oliver Cromwell; and like that between our fathers and the mother country, when the Declaration of Independence was put in issue. Some have originated in questions of form; some in the contentions of families; some in the fickleness of princes, and some in the machinations of politicians. England waged war on Holland, and one of the reasons openly assigned was an offensive picture in the town hall of Amsterdam. France hurled her armies across the Rhine, carrying fire and slaughter into the Palatinate, and involving great nations in a most bloody conflict, and all this wickedness has been traced to the intrigue of a minister, who sought in this way to divert the attention of his sovereign. But we are now in the midst of a war, which, whatever may be the reasons assigned by the unhappy men who began it, or by those who sympathize with them elsewhere, has an origin and main-spring so clear and definite as to be beyond question. Ideas are sometimes good and sometimes bad; and there may be a war for evil as well as for good. Such was that earliest rebellion waged by the fallen spirits against the Almighty Throne; and such, also, is that now waged by the fallen slave-masters of our Republic against the national Government.

If you will kindly listen, I shall now endeavor to unmask this rebellion, in its origin and main-spring. It is only when these are known that you can determine how the rebellion is to be treated. Your efforts will naturally be governed by the character of the adverse force—whether regarded as a motive power or as a disease. A steam-engine is stopped at once by stopping the steam. A ghastly cancer which has grappled the very fibres of the human frame, and shot its poison through every vein, will not yield to lip-salve or rose-water.

> Diseases desperate grown
> By desperate appliances are relieved,
> Or not at all.

On the 6th November last, the people of the United States, acting in pursuance of the Constitution and laws, chose Abraham Lincoln

President. Of course this choice was in every particular completely constitutional and legal. As such it was entitled to the respect and acquiescence of every good citizen. It is vain to say that the candidate represented opinions obnoxious to a considerable section of the country, or that he was chosen by votes confined to a special section. It is enough that he was duly chosen. You cannot set aside or deny such an election without assailing, not only the whole frame-work of the Constitution, but also the primal principle of American institutions. You become a traitor at once to the existing Government, and also to the very idea of popular rule. You snatch a principle from the red book of despotism, and openly substitute the cartridge-box for the ballot-box.

And yet, scarcely had this intelligence been flashed across the country, before the mutterings of sedition and treason began to reach us from the opposite quarter. The Union was menaced; and here the first distinct voice came from South Carolina. A Senator from that State, one of the largest slaveholders of the country, and a most strenuous partisan of slavery—Mr. Hammond—openly declared, in language not easily forgotten, that before the 18th December South Carolina would be "out of the Union high, and dry, and forever." These words heralded the outbreak. With the pertinacity of demons its leaders pushed forward. Their avowed object was the dismemberment of the Republic by detaching State after State, in order to found a slave-holding Confederacy. And here the clearest utterance came from a late Representative of Georgia—Mr. Stephens—now Vice-President of the rebel States, who did not hesitate to proclaim "that the foundations of the new Government are laid upon the great truth, that slavery—subordination to the superior race—is the negro's natural and moral condition; that it is the first Government in the history of the world based upon this great physical, philosophical, and moral truth; and that the stone which was rejected by the first builders is in the new edifice become *the chief stone of the corner*." Here is a savage frankness which shows an insensibility to shame. Surely the object avowed is hideous in every aspect, whether we regard it as treason to our paternal Government, as treason to the idea of American institutions, or as treason also to those commanding principles of economy, morals, and Christianity, without which civilization is changed into barbarism.

And now we stand face to face in deadly conflict with this double-headed, triple-headed treason. Beginning with those States most peculiarly interested in slavery, and operating always with an intensity proportioned to the prevalence of slavery, it has fastened upon other States less interested—Tennessee, North Carolina, Virginia—and with much difficulty has been prevented from enveloping every State containing slaves, no matter how few; for such is the malignant poison of slavery that only a few slaves will constitute a slave State with all the sympathies and animosities of slavery. This is the rebellion which I am to unmask. But bad as it is on its face, it becomes aggravated when we consider its origin, and the agencies by which it has been conducted. It is not merely a rebellion, but it is a rebellion begun in conspiracy; nor, in all history, ancient or modern, is there any record of conspiracy so vast and so wicked, ranging over such spaces both of time and territory, and contemplating such results. A conspiracy to seize a castle or to assassinate a prince is petty by the side of this enormous protracted treason, where half a continent studded with castles, fortresses, and public edifices, is seized, where the Government itself is overthrown, and where the President, on his way to the national capital, narrowly escaped a most cruel assassination.

But no conspiracy could have ripened into such wicked fruit, if it were not rooted in a soil of congenial malignity. To appreciate properly this influence, we must go back to the beginning of the Government.

South Carolina, which has taken so forward a part in this treason, hesitated originally, as is well known, with regard to the Declaration of Independence. Once her vote was recorded against that act; and when it finally prevailed, her vote was given for it only formally and for the sake of seeming unanimity. But so little was she inspired by the Declaration, that, in the contest which ensued, her commissioners made a proposition to the British commander, which has been properly characterized by an able historian as "equivalent to an offer from the State to return to the British crown." The same hesitation shown with regard to the Declaration of Independence was renewed with regard to the Federal Constitution, and here it was shared by another State. It is notorious that both South Carolina and Georgia, which, with the States carved out their original territory—Alabama and Mississippi—constitute the chief seat of the conspiracy—hesitated to become parties to the Union, and stipulated expressly for the recognition of the slave-trade in the Federal Constitution as an indispensable condition. In the Convention, Mr. Rutledge, of South Carolina, while opposing a tax on the importation of slaves, said: "The true question at present is, *whether Southern States* shall or shall not be parties to the Union." Mr. Pinckney, also of South Carolina, followed with the unblushing declaration: "South Carolina can never receive the plan [of the Constitution] *if it prohibits the slave-trade*." I quote now from Mr. Madison's authentic report of these important debates. (See Elliot's Debates, vol. v., p. 457.) With shame let it be confessed, that, instead of repelling this disgraceful overture, our fathers submitted to it, and in that submission you will find the beginning of our present sorrows. The slave-trade, whose aggregate iniquity no tongue can tell, was placed for twenty years under the safeguard of the Constitution, thus giving to slavery itself increase, support, and sanction. The language was modest, but the intent was complete. South Carolina and Georgia were pacified, and took their places in the Union, to which they were openly bound only by a most revolting tie. Regrets for the past are not entirely useless, if out of them we get wisdom for the future, and learn to be brave. It is easy now to see that, had the unnatural pretension of these States been originally encountered by a stern resistance worthy of an honest people, the present conspiracy would have been crushed before it saw the light. Its whole success, from its distant beginning down to this hour, has been from our timidity.

But there was also another sentiment, of a kindred perversity, which prevailed in the same quarter. This is vividly portrayed by John Adams, in a letter to General Gates, dated at Philadelphia, 23d March, 1776:

> "However, my dear friend Gates, all our misfortunes arise from a single source: *the resistance of the Southern colonies to Republican Government.*" * * * (John Adams' Works, vol. i., p. 207.)

And he proceeds to declare in strong language that "popular principles and axioms were abhorrent to the inclinations of the barons of the South." This letter was written in the early days of the Revolution. At a later period of his life John Adams testifies again to the discord between the North and the South; and he refers particularly to the period after the Federal Constitution, saying: "The Northern and the Southern States were invariably fixed in opposition to each other." (See letter to James Lloyd, 11th Feb., 1815, John Adams' Works, vol. x., p. 19.) This was before any question of tariff, or of free trade, or before the growing fortunes of the North had awakened Southern jealousy. The whole opposition had its root in slavery—as also had the earlier resistance to Republican Government.

In the face of these influences the Union was formed, but the seeds of conspiracy were latent in its bosom. The spirit already revealed was scarcely silenced; it was not destroyed. It still existed, rankling, festering, burning to make itself manifest. At the mention of slavery it always appeared full-armed, with barbarous pretensions. Even in the first Congress under the Constitution—at the presentation of that famous petition where Benjamin Franklin simply called upon Congress to step to the verge of its powers to discourage every species of traffic in our fellow-men—this spirit broke forth in violent threats. With a kindred lawlessness it early embraced that extravagant dogma of State rights which has been ever since the convenient cloak of treason and of conspiracy. At the Missouri question in 1820, it openly menaced a dissolution of the Union. Instead of throttling the monster, we submitted to feed it with new concessions. Meanwhile the conspiracy grew, until, at last, in 1830, under the influence of Mr. Calhoun, it assumed the defiant front of nullification; nor did it yield to the irresistible logic of Webster or the stern will of Jackson without a compromise. The pretended ground of complaint was the tariff; but Andrew Jackson, himself a patriot slaveholder—at that time President—saw the hollowness of the complaint. In a confidential letter, which has only recently been brought to light, dated at Washington, 1st May, 1833—and which, during the last winter, I had the honor of reading and holding up before the conspirators of the Senate, in the original autograph, he says:

> "The tariff was only the *pretext*, and disunion and a Southern Confederacy the real object. *The next pretext will be the negro or slavery question.*"

Jackson was undoubtedly right; but the pretext which he denounced in advance was employed so constantly afterwards as to become threadbare. At the earliest presentation of abolition petitions—at the Texas question—at the compromises of 1850—at the Kansas question—at the probable election of Fremont—on all these occasions, the Union was threatened by the angry slave-masters.

But the conspiracy has been unblushingly confessed by recent parties to it. Especially was this done in the rebel Convention of South Carolina.

Mr. Packer said: "Secession is no spasmodic effort that has come suddenly upon us. *It has been gradually culminating for a long series of years.*"

Mr. Inglis said: "Most of us have had this subject under consideration for *the last twenty years.*"

Mr. Keitt said: "I have been engaged in this movement *ever since I entered political life.*"

Mr. Rhett, who was in the Senate when I first entered that body, and did not hesitate then to avow himself a Disunionist, said, in the same Convention: "It is nothing produced by Mr. Lincoln's election or the non-execution of the fugitive slave law. *It is a matter which has been gathering head for thirty years.*"

The conspiracy thus exposed by Jackson and confessed by recent parties to it, was quickened by the growing passion for slavery throughout the slave States. The well-known opinions of the fathers, the declared convictions of all who were most eminent at the foundation of the Government, and the example of Washington were all discarded, and it was recklessly avowed that slavery is a divine institution—the highest type of civilization—a blessing to master and slave alike—and the very key-stone of our national arch. A generation has grown up with this teaching, so that it is now ready to say with Satan,

> Evil be thou my good; by thee at least
> Divided empire with heaven's king I hold;
> As man ere long and this new world shall know.

It is natural that a people thus trained should

listen to the voice of conspiracy. Slavery itself is a constant conspiracy, and its supporters, whether in the slave States or elsewhere, easily become indifferent to all rights and principles by which it may be constrained.

But this rage for slavery was itself quickened by two influences, which have shown themselves since the formation of our Union;—one economical and the other political. The first was found in the unexpected importance of the cotton-crop, which, through the labor of slaves and the genius of a New England inventor, has passed into an extraordinary element of wealth and of imagined strength, so that we have all been summoned to do homage to cotton as king. The second of these influences was found in the temptations of political power—than which no influence is more potent—for it became obvious that this power could be assured to slavery only through the permanent preponderance of its Representatives in the Senate; so that the continued control of all offices and honors was made to depend upon the extension of slavery. Thus, through two strong appetites—one for gain and the other for power—was slavery stimulated; but the conspiracy was strong only through slavery.

But even this conspiracy, thus supported and nurtured, would have been more wicked than strong, if it had not found perfidious aid in the very cabinet of the President. The Secretary of the Treasury, a slave-master from Georgia; the Secretary of the Interior, a slave-master from Mississippi; the Secretary of War, the notorious Floyd, a slave-master from Virginia; and, I fear, also the Secretary of the Navy, who was a Northern man with Southern principles, lent their active exertions. Through these eminent functionaries the treason was organized and directed, while their important posts were prostituted to its infamy. Here, again, you see the extent of the conspiracy. Never before, in any country, was there a similar crime, which embraced so many persons in the highest places of power, or which took within its grasp so large a theatre of human action. In anticipation of the election of Mr. Lincoln, the Cabinet conspirators had prepared the way for the rebellion:

First. The army of the United States was so far dispersed and exiled, that the commander-in-chief found it difficult during the recent anxious winter to bring together a thousand troops for the defence of the national capital, menaced by the conspirators.

Secondly. The navy was so far dispersed or dismantled, that on the 4th March, when the new Administration came into power, there were no ships to enforce the laws, collect the revenues, or protect the national property in the rebel ports. Out of 72 vessels of war, then counted as our navy, it appears that our whole available force at home was reduced to the steamer Brooklyn, carrying 25 guns, and the store-ship Relief, carrying 2 guns.

Thirdly. The forts on the extensive Southern coast were so far abandoned by the public force, that the larger part—counting upwards of 1,200 cannons, and built at a cost of upwards of six million dollars—became at once an easy prey to the rebels.

Fourthly. National arms were transferred from Northern to Southern arsenals, so as to disarm the free States and to equip the slave States. This was done on a large scale. Upwards of 115,000 arms, of the latest and most approved pattern, were transferred from the Springfield and Watervliet arsenals to different arsenals in the slave States, where they have been seized by the rebels. And a quarter of a million percussion muskets were sold to various slave States for $2.50 a musket, when they were worth, it is said, on an average, $12. Large quantities of cannon, mortars, powder, ball, and shell received the same direction.

Fifthly. The national Treasury, which so recently had been prosperous beyond example, was disorganized and plundered even to the verge of bankruptcy. Upwards of six millions are supposed to have been stolen, and much of this treasure doubtless went to help the work of rebellion.

Thus, even before its outbreak, the conspiracy contrived to degrade and despoil the Government, so as to secure a free course for the projected rebellion. The story seems incredible. But it was not enough to disperse the army, to disperse the navy, to abandon forts, to disarm the free States, and to rob the Treasury. The President of the United States, solemnly sworn to execute the laws, was won into a system of inactivity amounting to a practical abdication of his important trust. He saw treason plotting to stab at the heart of his country; he saw conspiracy, daily, hourly, putting on the harness of rebellion, but, though warned by the watchful commander-in-chief, he did nothing to arrest it, standing always

> —— like a painted Jove,
> With idle thunder in his lifted hand.

Aye, more; instead of those instant lightnings smiting and blasting in their fiery crash, which an indignant patriotism would have hurled at the criminals, he nodded sympathy and acquiescence. No page of history is more melancholy, because nowhere do we find a ruler who so completely abandoned his country; not Charles I. in his tyranny, not Louis XVI. in his weakness. Mr. Buchanan had been advanced to power by slave-masters, who knew well that he could be used for slavery. The slave-holding conspirators were encouraged to sit in his Cabinet, where they doubly betrayed their country, first by evil counsels, and then by disclosing what passed to their distant slave-holding confederates. The sudden act of Major Anderson, in removing from Fort Moultrie to Fort Sumter, and the sympathetic response of an aroused people, compelled a change of policy, and the rebellion received its first check. It was decided at last, after a painful struggle, that Fort Sumter should be maintained. It is difficult to exaggerate the importance of that decision, which, I believe, was duo mainly to an emient democrat—General Cass. This, at least, is true: it saved the national capital.

Meanwhile the conspiracy increased in activity, mastering State after State, gathering its forces and building its batteries. The time had come for the tragedy to begin. "At Nothingham," says the great English historian, speaking of King Charles I., "he erected his royal standard, the open signal of discord and civil war throughout the kingdom." The same open signal now came from Charleston, when tho conspirators ran up the rattle-snake flag, and directed their wicked cannonade upon the small, half-famished garrison of Sumter.

Were all this done in the name of revolution, or by virtue of any revolutionary principle, it would assume a familiar character. But this is not tho case. It is all done under the pretence of constitutional right. The forms of the Constitution are seized by the conspirators—as they have already seized every thing else—and wrested to the purposes of treason. It is audaciously declared that, under the existing Constitution, each State, in the exercise of its own discretion, may withdraw from the Union; and this asserted right of secession is invoked as the cover for a rebellion begun in conspiracy. The election of Mr. Lincoln is made the *occasion* for the exercise of this pretended right. Certain opinions at the North on the subject of slavery are made the *pretext.*

Who will not deny that this election can be a just *occasion?*

Who will not condemn the *pretext?*

But both occasion and pretext are determined by slavery, and thus testify to the part it has constantly performed.

And the pretended right of secession is not less monstrous than the pretext or the occasion; and this, too, testifies to slavery. It belongs to that brood of assumptions and perversions, of which slavery is the prolific parent. Wherever slavery prevails, this pretended right is recognized, and generally with an intensity proportioned to the prevalence of slavery; as, for instance, in South Carolina and Mississippi, more intensely than in Tennessee and Kentucky. It may be considered a fixed part of the slave-holding system. A pretended right to set aside the Constitution to the extent of breaking up the Government, is the natural companion of the pretended right to set aside human nature to the extent of making merchandise of men. They form a well-matched couple, and travel well together —destined to perish together. If we do not overflow toward the first with the same indignation which we feel for the latter, it is because its absurdity awakens our contempt. An English poet of the last century exclaims, in mocking verses—

> Crowned be the man with lasting praise,
> Who first contrived the pin,
> To loose mad horses from the chaise,
> And save the necks within.

But this is the impossible contrivance which has been attempted. Nothing is clearer than that this pretension, if acknowledged, leaves to every State the right to play at will "the mad horse," but with very little chance of saving any thing. It takes from the Government not merely the unity, but even the possibility of continued existence, and reduces it to the shadow of a name, or, at best, a mere tenancy at will—an unsubstantial form, liable to be decomposed at the touch of a single State. Of course, such an anarchical pretension—so instinct with all the lawlessness of slavery—must be encountered peremptorily. It is not enough to declare our dissent from it. We must see that our conduct is such as not to give it any recognition or foothold. [*Applause.*]

But instead of scouting this pretension, and utterly spurning it from the Government, new concessions to slavery were gravely propounded as the means of pacification—like a new sacrifice offered to an obscene divinity. It was argued that in this way the Border States at least might be preserved to the Union, and some of the Cotton States, perhaps, be won back to their duty; in other words, that in consideration of such concessions these States would consent to waive the present exercise of the pretended right of secession. Against all such propositions—without considering their character—there was on the threshold one obvious and imperative objection. It was clear that the very bargain or understanding, whether express or implied, was a recognition of this pretended right, and that a State yielding only to this appeal and detained through concessions, practically asserts this claim, and holds it for future exercise, *tanquam gladium in vagina.* Thus a concession called small becomes infinite, for it concedes the pretended right of secession and makes the permanence of the national Government impossible. Amidst all the grave responsibilities of the hour it belongs to us to take care that the life of the Republic is sacredly preserved. But this would be sacrificed at once, did we submit its existence to the conditions sought to be imposed.

But looking at the concessions proposed, I have always found them utterly unreasonable and indefensible. I should not expose them now, if they did not constantly testify to the origin and main-spring of this rebellion. Slavery was always the single subject-matter, and nothing else. Slavery was not only an integral part of every concession, but the single integer. The single idea was to give some new security—in some form—to slavery. That brilliant statesman, Mr. Canning, in one of those eloquent speeches which charm so much by the style, said that he was "tired of being a security-grinder," but his experience was not comparable to ours. "Security-grinding," in the name of slavery, has been for years the way in which we have encountered this conspiracy. [*Laughter and applause.*]

The propositions at the last Congress began with the President's Message, which in itself was one long concession. You do not forget his sympathetic portraiture of the disaffection throughout the Slave States, or his testimony to the cause. Notoriously and shamefully his heart was with the conspirators, and he knew intimately the main-spring of their conduct. He proposed nothing short of a general surrender to slavery, and thus did he proclaim slavery as the head and front—the very *causa causans*—of the whole crime.

You have not forgotten the Peace Conference—as it was delusively styled—convened at Washington on the summons of Virginia, with John Tyler in the chair, where New York as well as Massachusetts was represented by some of her ablest and most honored citizens. The sessions were with closed doors; but it is now known that throughout the proceedings, lasting for weeks, nothing was discussed but slavery. And the propositions finally adopted by the Convention were confined to slavery. Forbearing all details, it will be enough to say that they undertook to give to slavery positive protection in the Constitution, with new sanction and immunity—making it, notwithstanding the determination of our fathers, *national* instead of *sectional;* and even more than this, making it one of the essential and permanent parts of our republican system. But slavery is sometimes as deceptive as at other times it is bold; and these propositions were still further offensive from their studied uncertainty, amounting to positive duplicity. At a moment when frankness was needed above all things, we were treated to phrases pregnant with doubts and controversies, and were gravely asked, in the name of slavery, to embody them in the Constitution.

There was another string of propositions much discussed during the last winter, which bore the name of the venerable Senator from whom they came—Mr. Crittenden, of Kentucky. These also related to slavery and nothing else. They were more obnoxious even than those from the Peace Conference. And yet there were petitioners from the North—and even from Massachusetts—who prayed for this great surrender to slavery. Considering the character of these propositions—that they sought to change the Constitution in a manner revolting to the moral sense; to foist into the Constitution the idea of property in man; to protect slavery in all present territory south of 36° 30′, and to carry it into all territory hereafter acquired south of that line, and thus to make our beautiful Stars and Stripes in their southern march the flag of slavery; considering that they further sought to give new constitutional securities to slavery in the national capital and in other places within the exclusive Federal jurisdiction; that they sought to give new constitutional securities to the transit of slaves from State to State, opening the way to a roll-call of slaves at the foot of Bunker Hill or the gates of Faneuil Hall; and that they also sought the disfranchisement of more than 10,000 of my fellow-citizens in Massachusetts, whose rights are fixed by the Constitution of that Commonwealth, drawn by John Adams; considering these things, I felt at the time, and I still feel, that the best apology of these petitioners was that they were ignorant of the true character of these propositions, and that in signing the petition they knew not what they did. But even in their ignorance they testified to slavery, while the propositions were the familiar voice of slavery crying, "Give, give."

There was another single proposition which came from still another quarter, but like all the others, it related exclusively to slavery. It was to insert in the text of the Constitution a stipulation against any future amendment by which Congress might be authorized to interfere with slavery in the States. If you read this proposition you will find it crude and ill-shaped—a jargon of bad grammar—a jumble and hodge-podge of words—calculated to harmonize poorly with the accurate text of our Constitution. But even if tolerable in form, it was obnoxious, like the rest, as a fresh stipulation in favor of slavery. Sufficient surely in this respect is the actual Constitution. Beyond this I cannot, I will not, go. What Washington, Franklin, and Jay would not insert we cannot err in rejecting. [*Applause.*]

I do not dwell on other propositions, because they attracted less attention; and yet among these was one to overturn the glorious safeguards of freedom set up in the free States, known as the Personal Liberty Laws. Here again was slavery—with a vengeance. But there is one remark which I desire to make with regard to all these propositions. It was sometimes said that the concessions they offered to slavery were "small." What a mistake is this! No concession to slavery can be "small." Freedom is priceless, and in this simple rule alike of morals and jurisprudence, you will find the just measure of any concession, how small soever, by which freedom is sacrificed. Tell me not that it concerns a few only. I do not forget the saying of antiquity, that the best government is where an injury to a single individual is resented as an injury to the whole State; nor do I forget that memorable instance of our own recent history, where, in a distant sea, the thunders of our navy with all the hazards of war were aroused to protect the liberty of a solitary person who claimed the rights of an American citizen. By such examples let me be guided rather than by the suggestion that human freedom, whether in many or in few, is of so little value that it may be put in the market to appease a traitorous conspiracy or to soothe those who, without such concession, threaten to join the conspirators.

But the warnings of the past, like the suggestions of reason and of conscience, were all against concession. Timid counsels have always been an encouragement to sedition and rebellion. If the glove be of velvet, the hand must be of iron. An eminent master of thought, in some of his most vivid words, seems to have spoken for us. Here they are:

"To expect to tranquillize and benefit a country by gratifying its agitators, would be like the practice of the superstitious of old with their sympathetic powder and ointments; who, instead of applying medicaments to the wound, contented themselves with salving the sword which had inflicted it. Since the days of Dane-gelt downwards, nay, since the world was created, nothing but evil has resulted from concession made to intimidation."—*Whately's Essays of Bacon.* Essay 15, p. 134.

These words are most applicable to these times, when it has been so often proposed *to salve the sword of secession.*

In the same spirit spoke the most eminent practical statesman in English history, Mr. Fox. Here are his words:

"To humor the present disposition and temporize, is a certain, absolutely certain confirmation of the evil. No nation ever did or ever can recover from slavery by such methods."—*Charles James Fox, Letter to Lord Holland, 18th June,* 1804.

Pardon me if I express a regret, profound and heartfelt, that the pretensions of slavery, whether in its claim of privilege or in its doctrine of secession, were not always encountered boldly and austerely. Alas! it is ourselves that have encouraged the conspiracy and made it strong. Secession has become possible only through long-continued concession. In proposing concession we have encouraged secession, and while professing to uphold the Union, we have betrayed it. It seems now beyond question that the concessionists of the North have from the beginning played into the hands of the secessionists of the South. I do not speak in harshness or even in criticism, but simply according to my duty in unfolding historically the agencies, conscious and unconscious, which have been at work, while I hold them up as a warning for the future. They all testify to slavery, which from the earliest days has been at the bottom of the conspiracy and also at every stage of the efforts to arrest it. It was slavery which fired the conspirators, and slavery also which entered into every proposition of compromise. Secession and concession both had their root in slavery.

And now after this review, I am brought again to the significance of that Presidential election with which I began. The slave-masters entered into that election with Mr Breckinridge as their candidate, and their platform claimed constitutional protection for slavery in all Territories, whether now belonging to the Republic or hereafter acquired. This concession was the ultimatum on which was staked their continued loyalty to the Union—as the continuance of the slave-trade had been the original condition on which South Carolina and Georgia had entered into the Union. And the reason, though wicked, was obvious. It was because without such opportunity of expansion slavery would be stationary, while the Free States, increasing in number, would obtain a fixed preponderance in the national Government, assuring to them the political power. Thus at that election the banner of the slave-masters had for its open device—not the Union as it is, but the extension and perpetuation of human bondage. The popular vote was against further concession, and the conspirators proceeded with their crime. The *occasion* so long sought had come. The *pretext* foreseen by Jackson, was the motive power.

But here mark well that, in their whole conduct, the conspirators acted naturally under the instincts implanted by slavery; nay, they acted logically even. *Such is slavery that it cannot exist unless where it owns the government.* An injustice so plain can find protection only from a government which is a reflection of itself. Cannibalism cannot exist except under a government of cannibals. Idolatry cannot exist except under a government of idolaters. And Slavery cannot exist except under a government of slave-masters. This is positive, universal truth—at Petersburg, Constantinople, Timbuctoo, or Washington. The slave-masters of our country saw that they were dislodged from the national Government, and straightway they rebelled. The Republic which they could no longer rule they determined to ruin.

But though thus audaciously wicked, they are not strong in numbers. The whole quantity of slave-owners, great and small, according to the recent census, is not more than four hundred thousand; out of whom there are not more than one hundred thousand who are interested to any considerable extent in this peculiar species of property; and yet this petty oligarchy—itself controlled by a squad still more petty—in a population of many millions, has aroused and organized this gigantic rebellion. But this success is explained by two considerations. First, the asserted value of the slaves, reaching to the enormous sum total of two thousand millions of dollars, constitutes an overpowering property interest—one of the largest in the world; to which may be added the intensity and unity of purpose naturally belonging to the representatives of such a sum total, stimulated by the questionable character of the property. But, secondly, it is a phenomenon attested by the history of revolutions, that all such movements—at least in their early days—are controlled by minorities. This is because a revolutionary minority once embarked, has before it only the single simple path of unhesitating action. While others doubt or hold back, the minority strikes and goes forward. Audacity then counts more than numbers, and crime counts more than virtue. This phenomenon has been observed before. "Often have I reflected with awe," says Coleridge, "on the great and disproportionate power which an individual of no extraordinary talents or attainments may exert by merely throwing off all restraint of conscience. * * The abandonment of all *principle of right* enables the soul to choose and act upon a *principle of wrong*, and to subordinate to this one principle all the various vices of human nature."—(*Coleridge's Friend*, Essay 16.) These are remarkable words. But a French writer, Condorcet, the philosopher of the French Revolution, who sealed his principles by his death, urged this very phenomenon for a practical purpose. In a pamphlet addressed to the Parliamentary Reformers of England, he sought to enlist them in a revolutionary movement, and, by way of encouragement, he boldly announces that "revolutions must always be the work of the minority—that every revolution has been the work of a minority—that the French Revolution itself was accomplished by the minority." And Brissot de Warville, another partaker and victim also in this great Revolution, declared that it was carried by not more than twenty men. These declarations were made the subject of a debate shortly afterwards in the British Parliament, where Sheridan bore a brilliant part. They are most suggestive—even if they do not explain the early success of our conspirators. The future historian will record that the present rebellion—nowithstanding its protracted origin, the multitudes it has enlisted, and its extensive sweep—was at last precipitated by fewer than twenty men; Mr. Everett says by as few as ten. It is certain that thus far it has been the triumph of a minority; but of a minority moved, inspired, combined, and aggrandized by slavery.

And now this traitorous minority, putting aside all the lurking, slimy devices of conspiracy, steps forth in the full panoply of war. Assuming to itself all the functions of a government, it organizes States under a common head—sends ambassadors into foreign countries—levies taxes—borrows money—issues letters of marque—and sets armies in the field summoned from distant Georgia, Louisiana, and Texas, as well as from nearer Virginia, and composed of the whole lawless population—the poor who cannot own slaves as well as the rich who own them—throughout the extensive region where, with satanic grasp, this slaveholding minority claims for itself

—ample room and verge enough
The characters of hell to trace.

Pardon the language which I employ. The words of the poet do not picture too strongly the object proposed. And now these parricidal hosts stand arrayed openly against that paternal Government to which they owed loyalty, protection, and affection. Never in history did rebellion assume such a front. Call their numbers 400,000 or 200,000—what you will—they far surpass any armed forces ever before marshalled in rebellion; they are among the largest ever marshalled in war.

And all this is in the name of slavery, and for the sake of slavery, and at the bidding of slavery. The profligate favorite of the English monarch—the famous Duke of Buckingham—was not more exclusively supreme—even according to those words by which he was exposed to the judgment of his contemporaries—

Who rules the kingdom? The King.
Who rules the King? *The Duke.*
Who rules the Duke? The Devil.

The prevailing part here attributed to the royal favorite belongs now to slavery, which in the rebel States is a more than royal favorite.

Who rules the rebel States? The President.
Who rules the President? Slavery.
Who rules Slavery? ———

The latter question I need not answer. But all must see—and nobody can deny—that slavery is the ruling idea of this rebellion. It is slavery which marshals these hosts and breathes into their embattled ranks its own barbarous fire. It is slavery which stamps its character alike upon officers and men. It is slavery which inspires all, from the general to the trumpeter. It is slavery which speaks in the word of command and which sounds in the morning drum-beat. It is slavery which digs trenches and builds hostile forts. It is slavery which pitches its white tents and stations its sentries over against the national capital. It is slavery which sharpens the bayonet and casts the bullet; which points the cannon and scatters the shell, blazing, bursting with death. Wherever this rebellion shows itself—whatever form it takes—whatever thing it does—whatever it meditates—it is moved by slavery; nay, it is slavery itself, incarnate, living, acting, raging, robbing, murdering, according to the essential law of its being. [*Applause.*]

But this is not all. The rebellion is not only ruled by slavery, but owing to the peculiar condition of the slave States, it is for the moment, according to their boast, actually re-enforced by this institution. As the fields of the South are cultivated and labor generally is performed by slaves, the white freemen are at liberty to play the part of rebels. The slaves toil at home, while the masters work at rebellion, and thus by a singular fatality is this doomed race actually engaged, without taking up arms, in feeding, supporting, succoring, invigorating those who are now battling for their enslavement. Full well I know that this is an element of strength only through the indulgence of our own Government; but I speak now of things as they are; and that I may not seem to go too far, I ask your attention to the testimony of a Southern journal:

THE SLAVES AS A MILITARY ELEMENT IN THE SOUTH.—The total white population of the eleven States now comprising the Confederacy, is 6,000,000, and, therefore, to fill up the ranks of the proposed army, (600,000,) about ten per cent. of the entire white population will be required. In any other country than our own, such a draft could not be met, but the Southern States can furnish that number of men and still not leave the material interests of the country in a suffering condition. Those who are incapacitated for bearing arms can oversee the plantations, and *the negroes can go on undisturbed in their usual labors.* In the North the case is different; the men who join the army of subjugation are the laborers, the producers, and the factory operatives. Nearly every man from that section, especially those from the rural districts, leaves some branch of industry to suffer during his absence. *The institution of slavery in the South alone enables her to place in the field a force much larger in proportion to her white population than the North,* or indeed any country which is dependent entirely on free labor. The institution is a tower of strength to the South, *particularly at the present crisis,* and our enemies will be likely to find that the "moral cancer," about which their orators are so fond of prating, is really *one of the most effective weapons employed against the Union by the South.* Whatever number of men may be needed for this war, we are confident our people stand ready to furnish. We are all enlisted for the war, and there must be no holding back until the independence of the South is fully acknowledged.—*Montgomery* (*Ala.*) *Advertiser.*

As the rebels have already confessed the conspiracy which led to the rebellion, so in this article do they openly confess the main-spring of their strength. With triumphant vaunt, they declare slavery to be the especial source of their belligerent power.

But slavery may be seen not only in what it has done for the rebellion of which it is the indisputable head—the fountain and life—but also in what it has inflicted upon us. There is not a community, not a family, not an individual, man, woman, or child, who does not feel its heavy, bloody hand. Why these mustering armies? Why this drum-beat in your peaceful streets? Why these gathering means of war? Why these swelling taxes? Why these unprecedented loans? Why this derangement of business? Why among us the suspension of the *habeas corpus,* and the prostration of all safeguards of freedom? Why this constant solicitude visible in all your faces? The answer is clear. Slavery is the author, the agent, the cause. The anxious hours that you pass are darkened by slavery. The *habeas corpus,* and all those safeguards of freedom which you deplore have been prostrated by slavery. The business which you have lost has been filched by slavery. The millions of money now amassed by patriotic offerings are all snatched by slavery. The taxes now wrung out of your diminished means are all consumed by slavery. And all these gathering means of war—this drum-beat in your peaceful streets—and these mustering armies—are on account of slavery and nothing else. Do the poor feel constrained to forego their customary tea, or coffee, or sugar, now burdened by increased taxation? let them pledge themselves anew against the criminal giant tax-gatherer. Does any community mourn gallant men, who, going forth joyous and proud beneath their country's flag, have been brought home cold and stiff, with its folds wrapped about them for a shroud? Let all who truly mourn the dead be aroused against slavery. Does a mother drop tears for a son in the flower of his days cut down upon the distant battle-field which he moistens with his youthful, generous blood? Let her know that slavery dealt the deadly blow which took at once his life and her peace. [*Sensation.*]

But I hear a voice saying that all this proceeds not from slavery—oh no!—but from anti-slavery; that the Republicans, who hate slavery,—that the Abolitionists—are the authors of this terrible conflagration. Surely you may well suspect the sense or loyalty of him who puts forth this irrational and utterly wicked imputation. As well say that the early Christians were the authors of the heathen enormities against which they bore their martyr testimony, and that the cross, the axe, the gridiron, and the boiling oil by which they suffered were a part of the Christian dispensation. But the early Christians were misrepresented and falsely charged with crime, even as you are. The tyrant Nero, after setting Rome on fire and dancing at the conflagration, denounced the Christians as guilty of this wickedness. Here are the authentic words of the historian Tacitus:

"So for the quieting of this rumor, Nero judicially charged with the crime, and punished with most studied severities, that class, hated for their general wickedness, whom the vulgar call Christians. The originator of that name was one Christ, who, in the reign of Tiberius, suffered death by sentence of the procurator Pontius Pilate. The baneful superstition, thereby repressed for the time, again broke out, not only over Judea, the native soil of that mischief, but in the city also, where from every side all atrocious and abominable things collect and flourish." (*Annal.* XV. 44.)

The writer of these remarkable words was the wisest and most penetrating man of his generation, and he lived amidst the events which he describes. Perhaps in listening to him you may find an apology for those among us who heap upon contemporaries a similar obloquy. The Abolitionists need no defence from me. It is to their praise—destined to fill an immortal page—that from the beginning they saw the true character of slavery and warned their country against its threatening domination. Through them the fires of liberty have been kept alive in the United States—as Hume is constrained to confess that these same fires were kept alive in England by the Puritans, whom this great historian never praised if he could help it. And yet they are charged with this rebellion. Can this be serious? Even at the beginning of the Republic the seeds of the conspiracy were planted, and in

1820, and then again in 1830, it showed itself—while nearly thirty years ago Jackson denounced it, and one of its leading spirits has recently boasted that it has been gathering head for this full time, thus—not only in its distant embryo, but in its well-attested development—ante-dating those Abolitionists whose prophetic patriotism is now made the apology for the crime. As well, where the prudent passenger has warned the ship's crew of the fatal lee-shore, arraign him for the wreck which has engulfed all; as well cry out that the philosopher who foresees the storm is responsible for the desolation that ensues, or that the astronomer who calculates the eclipse is the author of the darkness which covers the earth. [*Enthusiastic applause.*]

And now, that I may give a practical character to this whole history, let me bring it all to bear upon our present situation and its duties. You have seen Slavery even before the Federal Union, not only a disturbing influence, but an actual bar to Union except on condition of surrender to its immoral behests. You have seen Slavery at all times militant whenever any proposition was brought forward with regard to it, and more than once threatening a dissolution of the Union. You have seen Slavery for many years the animating principle of a conspiracy against the Union, while it matured its flagitious plans and obtained the mastery of Cabinet and President. And when the conspiracy had wickedly ripened, you have seen that it was only by concessions to Slavery, that it was encountered, as by similar concessions it had from the beginning been encouraged. You now see Rebellion everywhere throughout the Slave States elevating its bloody crest and threatening the existence of the National Government, and all in the name of Slavery, while it proposes to establish a new government whose corner-stone shall be Slavery. [*Hisses, and cries of Never!*]

Against this rebellion we wage war. It is our determination, as it is our duty, to crush it; and this will be done. The region now contested by the rebels belongs to the United States by every tie of government and of right. Some of it has been bought by our money, while all of it—with its rivers, harbors, and extensive coast—has become essential to our business in peace and to our defence in war. Union is a geographical—economical—commercial—political—military—and if I may so say—even a fluvial necessity. Without union, peace on this continent is impossible; but life without peace is impossible also.

Only by crushing this rebellion can union and peace be restored. Let this be seen in its reality, and who can hesitate? If this were done instantly—without further contest—then besides all the countless advantages of every kind obtained by such restoration, two especial goods will be accomplished—one political and the other moral as well as political. First, the pretended right of secession, with the whole pestilent extravagance of State Sovereignty, which has supplied the machinery for this rebellion and afforded a delusive cover for treason, will be trampled out—never again to disturb the majestic unity of the republic. And, secondly, the unrighteous attempt to organize a new confederacy solely for the sake of slavery and with slavery as its corner-stone, will be overthrown. These two pretensions, one so shocking to our reason and the other so shocking to our moral nature, will disappear forever. And with their disappearance will commence a new epoch, the beginning of a grander period. But if by any accident the rebellion should prevail, then just in proportion to its triumph, whether through concession on our part, or through successful force on the other part, will the Union be impaired and peace be impossible. Therefore, in the name of the Union and for the sake of peace are you summoned to the work.

But how shall the rebellion be crushed? That is the question. Men, money, munitions of war, a well-supplied commissariat, means of transportation;—all these you have in abundance—in some particulars beyond the rebels. You have too the consciousness of a good cause, which in itself is an army. And yet thus far—until within a few days—the advantage has not been on our side. The explanation is easy. The rebels are combating at home on their own soil, strengthened and maddened by Slavery, which is to them an ally and a fanaticism. More thoroughly aroused than ourselves—more terribly in earnest—with every sinew vindictively strained to its most perfect work—they freely use all the resources that God and nature put into their hands; raising against us, not only the whole white population, but enlisting the war-whoop of the Indians—cruising upon the sea in pirate ships to despoil our commerce and, at one swoop, confiscating our property to the extent of hundreds of millions of dollars, while all this time their four millions of slaves undisturbed at home are freely contributing by their labor to sustain the war, which without them must soon expire.

It remains for us to encounter the rebellion calmly and surely by a force superior to its own. But to this end something more will be needed than men or money. Our battalions must be reënforced by ideas, and we must strike directly at the origin and main-spring of the rebellion. I do not say now in what way or to what extent; but simply that we must strike; it may be by the system of a Massachusetts General—Butler; it may be by that of Fremont, [*here the audience rose and gave long-continued cheers;*] or it may be by the grander system of John Quincy Adams. Reason and sentiment both concur in this policy, which is only according to the most common principles of human conduct. In no way can we do so much at so little cost. To the enemy such a blow will be terror; to good men it will be an encouragement, and to foreign nations watching this contest, it will be an earnest of something beyond a mere carnival of battle. There has been the cry "On to Richmond," and still another worse cry "On to England." Better than either is the cry, "On to Freedom." [*Tremendous cheering.*] Let this be heard in the voices of your soldiers; aye—let it resound in the purposes of the Government, and victory must be ours. By this sign conquer.

It is with no little happiness that I now announce that this cry is at last adopted by the Government. You will find it in the instructions from the Secretary of War, dated War Department, Oct. 14th, 1861, and addressed to the general commanding the forces which have just effected a successful landing in South Carolina. Here are the important words:

"You will, however, in general avail yourself of the services of any persons, whether fugitives from labor or not, who may offer them to the National Government; you will employ such persons in such services as they may be fitted for, either as ordinary employees or, if special circumstances seem to require it, in any other capacity, with such organization, in squads, companies or otherwise, as you deem most beneficial to the service. This, however, not to mean a general arming of them for military service. You will assure all loyal masters that Congress will provide just compensation to them for the loss of the services of the persons so employed."

These words have not the positive form of a proclamation; but, analyze them, and you will find them full of meaning. First, martial law is hereby declared; for the powers committed to the discretion of the general are derived from that law and not from the late Confiscation Act of Congress. Secondly, fugitive slaves are not to be surrendered. Thirdly, all coming within the camp are to be treated as freemen. Fourthly, they may be employed in such service as they may be fitted for. Fifthly, in squads, companies or otherwise, with the single limitation that this is not to mean "a *general* arming of them for military service." And, sixthly, compensation, through Congress, is promised to loyal masters; saying nothing of rebel masters. All this is little short of a Proclamation of Emancipation—not unlike that of old Caius Marius, when he landed on the coast of Etruria, and, according to Plutarch, proclaimed liberty to the slaves. As such I do not err when I call it the most important event of the war—the more important because it is understood to have the deliberate sanction of the President as well as of the Secretary of War, and therefore marks the policy of the Administration. That this policy should be first applied to South Carolina is just. As the great rebellion began in this State, so should the great remedy. [*Applause and cheers.*]

Slavery is the inveterate culprit—the transcendent criminal—the persevering traitor—the arch rebel—the open outlaw. As the less is contained in the greater, so the rebellion is all contained in Slavery. The tenderness which you show to Slavery is, therefore, tenderness to the rebellion itself. [*Applause.*] The pious caution with which you avoid harming Slavery is like that ancient superstition, which made the wolf sacred among the Romans and the crocodile sacred among the Egyptians; nor shall I hesitate to declare that every surrender of a slave by your soldiers back to bondage is an offering of human sacrifice—whose shame is too great for any army to bear. That men should still hesitate to strike at Slavery is only another illustration of human weakness. The English republicans, in their bloody contest with the Crown, hesitated for a long time to fire upon the king; but under the valiant lead of Cromwell, surrounded by his well-trained Ironsides, they banished all such scruple, and you know well the result. The king was not shot, but his head was brought to the block.

The duty which I suggest, if not urgent now, as a MILITARY NECESSITY, *in just self-defence*, will present itself constantly on other grounds, *as our armies advance in the Slave States or land on their coasts.* If it does not stare us in the face at this moment, it is because unhappily we are still everywhere on the defensive. As we begin to be successful it must rise before us for practical decision; and you cannot avoid it. There will be slaves in your camps or within your extended lines whose condition you must determine. There will be slaves also claimed by rebels, whose continued chattelhood you will scorn to recognize. The decision of these two cases will settle the whole great question. Nor can the rebels complain. They challenge our armies to enter upon their territory in the free exercise of all the powers of war—according to which, as you well know, all private interests are subordinated to the public safety, which for the time becomes the supreme law above all other laws and above the Constitution itself. If everywhere under the flag of the Union,—in its triumphant march,—Freedom is substituted for Slavery, this outrageous rebellion will not be the first instance in history where God has turned the wickedness of man into a blessing; nor will the example of Samson stand alone when he gathered honey out of the carcass of the dead and rotten lion. [*Cheers.*]

Pardon me if I speak only in hints, and do not stop to argue or explain. Not now, at the close of an address, devoted to the rebellion in its origin and main-spring, can I enter upon this great question of military duty in its details. There is another place where this discussion will be open for me. [*Cheers.*] It is enough now if I indicate the simple principle which will be the natural guide of all who are really in earnest—of all whose desire to save their country is stronger than their desire to save Slavery. You will strike where the blow will be most felt; nor will you miss the precious opportunity. The enemy is before you; nay he has come out in ostentatious challenge, and his name is Slavery. You can vindicate the Union only by his prostration. Slavery is the very Goliah of the rebellion, armed with a coat of mail, with a helmet of brass upon his head, greaves of brass upon his legs, a target of brass between his shoulders, and with the staff of his spear like a weaver's beam. But a stone from a simple sling will make the giant fall upon his face to the earth. [*Prolonged cheering.*]

Thank God! our Government is strong; but thus far all signs denote that it is not strong enough to save the Union and at the same time to save slavery. One or the other must suffer; and just in proportion as you reach forth to protect slavery, do you protect this accursed rebellion; nay, you give to it that very aid and comfort, which under our Constitution is treason itself. Perversely and pitifully do you postpone that sure period of reconciliation, not only between the two sections—not only between the men of the North and the men of the South, but, more beautiful still, between the slave and his master, without which that true tranquillity, which we all seek, cannot be permanently assured to our country. Believe it; only through such reconciliation, under the sanction of Freedom, can you remove all occasion of contention hereafter; only in this way, can you cut off the head of this great rebellion, and at the same time extirpate that principle of evil, which, if allowed to remain, must shoot forth in perpetual discord, if not in other rebellions; only in this way can you command that safe victory—without which this contest will be vain—which will have among its conquests Indemnity for the Past and Security for the Future—the noblest indemnity and the strongest security ever won—because founded in the redemption of a race. [*Cheers.*]

Full well I know the doubts, cavils, and misrepresentations to which this argument for the integrity of our Government is exposed; but I turn with confidence to the people. The heart of the people is right, and all great thoughts come from the heart. All who hate Slavery and who are true to Freedom will join instinctively in this effort, paying with person, time, talent, purse. They are the minute men of this war—always ready; and yet more ready just in proportion as the war is truly inspired. They at least are sure. It only remains that others who do not share in this animosity to Slavery—that merchants who study their legers—that bankers who study their discounts—and that politicans who study success—should see that only by a prompt and united effort against Slavery can this war be brought to a speedy and triumphant close, without which merchant, banker, and politician will all suffer alike. Leger, discount, and political aspiration will be of small value if the war continues its lava flood, shrivelling and stifling every thing but itself. Therefore, *under the spur of self-interest, if not under the necessities of self-defence*, we must act together. Humanity too joins in this appeal. Blood enough has been already shed—victims enough have been offered at the altar—even if you are willing to continue to Slavery the tribute we are now paying of more than a million of dollars a day.

Events too, under Providence, will be our masters. For the rebels there can be no success. Every road for them leads to disaster. Defeat for them will be bad; but victory will be worse; for then will the North be inspired to a sublimer energy. The proposition of emancipation which shook ancient Athens followed close upon the disaster at Cheronœa; and the statesman who moved it afterwards vindicated himself by saying that it proceeded not from him but from Cheronœa. The Act of Congress punishing the rebels by giving freedom to their slaves *employed against us*—familiarly known as the Confiscation Act—passed the Senate on the morning after the disaster at Manassas. In the providence of God there are no accidents; and this seeming reverse thus helped the way to the greatest victory which can be won.

There is a classical story of a mighty hunter, whose life in the Book of Fate, had been made to depend upon the preservation of a brand which was burning at his birth. The brand, so full of destiny, was snatched from the flames and carefully preserved by his prudent mother. Meanwhile the hunter became powerful and invulnerable to mortal weapons. But at length the mother, indignant at his cruelty to her own family, flung the brand upon the flames and the hunter died. The story of that hunter, so powerful and invulnerable to mortal weapons, is now repeated in this rebellion, and Slavery is the fatal brand. Let our Government, which has thus far preserved Slavery with maternal care, simply fling it upon the flames which itself has madly aroused, and the rebellion will die at once. [*Sensation.*]

Amidst all the perils which now surround us, there is one only which I dread. It is the peril which comes from some new surrender to Slavery—some fresh recognition of its power—some present dalliance with its intolerable pretensions. Worse than any defeat or even the flight of an army would be such abandonment of principle. From all such peril, good Lord deliver us! And there is *one way of safety*, clear as sunlight—pleasant as the paths of Peace. Over its broad and open gate is written simply, JUSTICE. There is victory in that word. Do justice, and you will be twice-blessed; for so you will subdue the rebel master while you elevate the slave. Do justice frankly, generously, nobly, and you will find strength instead of weakness, while all seeming responsibility will disappear in obedience to God's everlasting law. Do justice, though the Heavens fall; but they will not fall. Every act of justice becomes a new pillar of the Universe, or it may be a new link of that

——————golden everlasting chain
Whose strong embrace holds heaven and earth and main.

www.ingramcontent.com/pod-product-compliance
Lightning Source LLC
LaVergne TN
LVHW010834120826
845149LV00016B/1371

* 9 7 8 1 4 1 8 1 9 0 1 2 5 *